FU★K
YOUR
CANOES

FU★K YOUR CANOES

PAVING YOUR OWN PATH

JOHN DOERR

ISBN: 978-0-578-92234-8

CONTENTS

INTRODUCTION

A construction worker, an MMA fighter, and a US Marine are on a plane when it crash-lands in the Amazon forest. They are promptly captured by an unknown cannibal tribe who informs the three men that they will be killed and eaten, and their skin will be used to make the tribe's canoes. Then they are each given a final request. The construction worker asks to be killed as quickly and painlessly as possible. So, they give him a poisonous frog to eat. He eats it and dies instantly. Thinking it would be quick and painless, the MMA fighter asks to be shot, so they shoot him dead and save his skin for their canoes. Now it's the Marine's turn. He asks for a simple dinner fork. The cannibals are confused, but they reluctantly provide him with a fork. As soon as he has the fork, he begins stabbing himself in the legs, arms, belly, and back. He's bleeding from all the small wounds, but he is not dying. After twenty minutes of this, the cannibal chieftain asks in an angry voice, "What the hell are you doing?!?" To which the Marine replies with a finger in the air, "FUCK YOUR CANOES!"

No matter how messed up your situation is, and no matter how many times you fail, you can ALWAYS affect your own outcome for the better. I have lived my entire adult life by the simple concept and belief that we are ALL born with a million dollars in our head and in our ass! It's up to us to get it out.

This book will teach you how to look at your life, improve your relationships, and get the money that you have earned!

This life doesn't owe you ANYTHING, for life is an unfair, heartless, unfeeling, Machiavellian that would just as soon chew you up and spit you out as look at 'ya. This book will teach you how to change your life by employing a simple set of guidelines to be successful. They are short and EASY to remember.

As an American male, a husband, a father of three, a former Marine Corps Sergeant, an inventor, and now a heavy civil construction manager, I've learned that having the right attitude is the number-one key to success.

How did a guy who started out as a poor farm boy from Florida with a learning disability grow up to be honorably discharged from the United States Marine Corps, graduate cum laude with a bachelor of science in building construction from the University of North Florida, become successful professionally, patent an invention, and write a book? Well, it's partly because I have a problem with authority, and I don't like being told "no" or being limited by what I'm told to do. (The irony of having a problem with authority and becoming a US Marine is not lost on me.) But the most important element of my success is that I've developed the right attitude in everything I do, and I OUT-WORK almost everyone I know.

Men, our job is SIMPLE: We are here to create opportunity, build our self-esteem, and provide for our families. We are required to be successful and SHOW UP to be the best man, husband, father, and protector we can be. It can be easy to get it right, but it's also easy to fuck it up. (Honestly, it's the women who have the tough job.)

You need to have the right attitude to succeed. It is not pride, hatred, nor anger that compels us to succeed; it's an unapologetically cocky and focused attitude coupled with the willingness to do what the other guy will not. This is what always wins out in the end.

Unfortunately, society's messaging doesn't always point us in the right direction. A guy cannot turn on the TV or pick up a paper without being bombarded by negative imagery and self-defeating phrases designed to prevent us from being whom and what we are destined to be. This book attempts to change all of that by shedding light on five key guidelines to help you affect positive change in your life.

I'll show you how to overcome any obstacle so you can reach your goals. The right attitude requires one to, "know what a man CAN DO and what a man CAN'T DO." (Thanks to Captain Jack Sparrow for that wisdom.) This is life's one and only true *rule*. This simple statement allows us to flank and overcome every perceived or actual roadblock we might fall victim to. If the proverbial door is closed, if your path is blocked, or if you're in a stalemate and don't know what to do, you need to home in on what you CAN control and think outside the fucking box. In Marines terms, thinking outside the box is the embodiment of saying, "Wait, are you telling *me* I can't open that door? 'Cause I'll be right back with my Mark 19* and open us a 'door' from 1,500 yards away!"

I'll also show you how to grow your relationships, surround yourself with the right people, and learn to trust those who deserve to be trusted.

---

* A Mark 19 (Mk 19) is a belt-fed 40 mm grenade launcher that sits on a tripod or can be vehicle-mounted and necessarily constitutes shit-tons of mobile firepower.

Roadblocks can stop us from reaching our goals, but they are easily undermined and blown to shit by applying the guidelines in this book.

I am here to tell you that regardless of who you are or where you came from, if you adopt this model of success, the sky's the limit, except that Elon Musk just raised that bar when he shot an electric sports car at the planet Mars. Take a second to think about that: Elon Musk—a bullied kid from a divorced home who came to the United States with almost no money—just launched his own rocket with his own electric vehicle on it into the Martian orbit, and in doing so he singlehandedly ruined the phrase "the sky's the limit." (He's probably sitting around right now drinking a beer and thinking of other cool phrases to fucking destroy, but I digress.) Without question, Elon Musk understood what he could do and what he couldn't do, and he is an unapologetic embodiment of creating his own measure of success. What limits will YOU obliterate when you reach your full potential?

WHAT A MAN CAN DO AND WHAT A MAN CAN'T DO

This book will not get into a bunch of Tony Robbins "unlock your inner potential" bullshit, nor will it Dr. Phil it all up with "get-real" statements. This is a simple set of five guidelines you can apply to your life in order to set your mind up for success. Employ them however you want for your own life and fit them to your individual situation.

GUIDELINE #1: "NO" NEVER MEANS "NO."

Now, before you go all #metoo and spin this guideline like a fucking rotisserie chicken, this author has a wife and two daughters at home, so trust me when I say there is really only one set of circumstances where "no" does actually mean "no." (Hence why I own several shotguns and learned how to operate heavy equipment.) What it does mean, in the context of this guideline, is that when you are told the words "no," "can't," or "impossible," you need to figure out how to flank that position, find another way, and keep moving forward to turn that "no" into a "did you just see that shit?!"

For example, Barney Ford, an escaped black slave, moved to Breckenridge, Colorado, in 1860 to try his hand at gold mining. Because Ford was a black man, in order to stake his claim, he had to form a contract with a white Denver lawyer who demanded 20 percent of his profits. After Ford found copious amounts of gold, that same lawyer used the law to have Ford evicted from his house and took the claim for himself. Ford was literally run out of town and was told "no" by a gang of men with guns. Ford then moved to Denver, Colorado, where he opened up a hotel, and then he opened another hotel in Cheyenne, Wyoming. Unfortunately, he went broke in those ventures, too, and the market told him "no" in a colossal way. Barney then headed back to Breckenridge in 1880 and rented a small part of a building downtown where he started a restaurant called Ford's Chop House, which ultimately provided him the financial ability to buy the entire building and then—no shit—an entire city block downtown. He ended up building the finest house in town on that block. Barney, the former slave who was called every name in the book, was swindled out of his fortune, went broke, got run out of town, and still came out on top. He flanked all the adversity and overcame being told "no." He ended life richer and more successful than every other guy in the town because he did not take "no" for an answer.

In other words, **don't stop moving forward, dammit**. Keep problem solving, go all-in, and keep trying to find a way through. Don't be afraid to fail along the way. Failure can feel like a big "no" being thrown at you, but as long as you analyze how you failed, know it, and understand it, you will not make that same mistake again.

Simply put, when you fail and learn from it, it's called a mistake; however, when you fail and don't learn from, only then is it a true failure.

Don't wait for others to give you permission during the process. It is nice when people like what you are doing, but that should **never guide**

your decision. Create your own path to get around any "no," and don't look back at what others think of you. Know this: You will be judged by others regardless of what you do. WHO CARES?! **I'm sorry that I am not sorry.** I seriously do not give a shit about anyone's opinion when I make a decision because I'm the one in the trenches, carving my own way.

Gentlemen, to be successful you need to be able to move past a "no" and go forward confidently, without caring what others think. When Barney Ford was run out of town and sought success elsewhere, he didn't dwell on the opinions of the guys who chased him out at gunpoint. If he had, he never would have gone on to make his fortune. Take a cue from Ford and keep moving forward. WHO CARES what anyone thinks? If they harbor good will or ill will toward you, it's on them. If they love you or hate you, it's on them. Whether they see your vision or think you're insane, it is **ON THEM**. You MUST keep moving forward regardless. You will leave some people behind, piss some people off, and ruffle some feathers, but you'll also bring others happiness, joy, and opportunity.

You are building your own life and striving for success for YOU, not for them.

GUIDELINE #2: WORK HARD TO GET LUCKY.

We are not talking about Hugh Hefner or Tiger Woods here, gents (although they arguably did work hard to get lucky). We're talking about putting in the effort to create your own luck.

Before I started working at Barnard Construction Company, I was asked to go to Bozeman, Montana, for training.

During the training, the CEO, Tim Barnard, looked at me and said, "The harder I work the luckier I get. What does that mean, John?"

I simply replied, "I don't know, sir. I don't believe in luck."

Now, I was in corporate training. I was the "Friggin' New Guy" (FNG), and I just seemingly popped off as a smart-ass to the Chief Executive Officer of one of the "Top 400 Contractors" named by *Engineering News-Record* (ENR).

With some surprise and confusion, he asked me to elaborate, so I did. I said, "I believe that what people call 'luck' is where hard work and preparation meet on the demand curve." (My macroeconomics professor taught me that.) It turned out that was Tim's point all along.

But wait, John. I know a guy who bought a scratch-off ticket and won $10,000. And I know a guy who pulled a lever in Vegas and won $20,000. Okay, that is just dumb luck. Same goes if you are walking down the street and you spot a $20 bill on the ground; that is also "luck." But that kind of luck will break a man should he pursue it, and it will NOT allow you to achieve any type of goal, let alone feed and clothe your family. Opportunity doesn't just come knocking at your door. There is no mystical force called "opportunity" that is just waiting to strike you. There is not a finite amount of opportunity that can be taken from you and hoarded by your successful neighbor. **You are the opportunity! You MAKE the opportunity happen** by carving it out of yourself with your grit and your determination.

In the 1950s, my grandfather, John Fichera, moved his family from New Jersey to Pompano Beach, Florida, where he started two farms. One of his farms was located in Delray Beach and the other was about twelve miles south in an area of Boca Raton that the locals called "the rock pit." Not a man to be deterred, he cleared the land, set up the irrigation, and removed the rocks from his "rock pit." He then sold the rocks to a local concrete plant.

Later, when he produced more class-A peppers than any other farm in the state per yield, a rep from the University of Florida's Institute of Food and Agricultural Sciences paid him a visit to find out how he did it. He told the rep he sprayed his fields with a mixture of 50 percent copper and 50 percent Manzate fungicide. The copper keeps the leaves tough during hard Florida rains and the humid environment requires that much Manzate to prevent the crops from rotting in the field. The rep mocked him and said he was wasting his time and money. Nevertheless, two years later, that same spray mixture became the state standard for the next twenty or so years.

Once again, John Fichera was mocked when he told the Pompano Farmers Market that he planned to plant cucumbers. Up until that point, most of the cucumbers had been grown and imported into Florida from the Bahamas because Florida soil could not support or sustain the nutrients required to profitably grow cucumbers. Well, he quintupled the amount of fertilizer, adjusted his irrigation, and set the market price* that year. In fact, he was the only Florida farmer to produce cucumbers that year and, in his words, he "pretty-near† needed to hire a man just to count the money" he made.

The point is, John Fichera was not lucky! He worked hard, he was analytical about his goals, and he problem-solved his way to success. He

---

* Set the market: When a supplier has an abundance or is the only supplier of a product, he/she can set his or her price for their goods. Another way of saying this is for one to "corner the market."

† Pretty-near: A vernacular holdover from the 1940s that Fichera used, which means "almost" today.

understood that "no" doesn't always mean "no," and he didn't fall for the illusion of luck. He figured out a way to make his crops grow better than anyone else's in the state. He did not wait for opportunity to knock at his door; **he was that opportunity.** Fichera never went to high school and he had no formal education of any sort, but he still went on to become one of the most successful farmers in the state of Florida for his farm-size. He literally cut and cleared his way into prosperity, and he ended up being a multi-millionaire. Cha-ching!

GUIDELINE #3: REMOVE DISTRACTIONS.

In the Introduction of this book, I mentioned that our society has made it easy to adopt a self-defeating lifestyle and mindset. And one of the most common ways that happens is by getting distracted by our phones and social media. When it comes to achieving your goals, you need to remove those distractions and focus on what really matters.

It's a simple concept. Take Gordon Ramsay, for example. By his own admission, Ramsay failed at his first restaurant and came back at it a second time to achieve great success and has never looked back. When was the last time you saw that man on his cell phone or computer? He doesn't need to put down his phone to tell someone they are a STUPID DONKEY because he's **not on his fucking cell phone.** When he is working and telling people how "shitty" they are or that their "salmon looks like a bison's penis," he is not surfing the internet, playing Candy Crush, or swiping right or left on his cell phone. He is focused on maintaining his standards, promoting his businesses, and moving in new directions.

Every action Ramsay takes is in a relentless pursuit of quality, success, and money. He never takes "no" for an answer. He works harder than

99 percent of the population to create his own opportunity. And, most importantly he is NOT DISTRACTED by whoever just posted a clip of cats being afraid of cucumbers on Facebook*.

Look, removing distractions doesn't mean you should become a workaholic, but it does mean you should limit how often you log into Facebook and Twitter, and turn off updates for any pages that are not helping you to be productive. You may also need to limit video game playing to once a week or until after your responsibilities are done for the day. You should also limit how much time you spend with fun yet distracting people. Go hang out at the bar with your friends, but limit that stuff to once a month. If they are your true friends, they will understand the cutback on your time spent with them. Stay away from fucking drugs, too. Oh, I can hear it now... *John, I know a guy who smokes a pound of weed every week and he is super successful.* Yeah, I know two, and their names are Snoop Doggy Dogg and Willie Nelson (see guideline #2 above).†

The same goes for staying focused while you are on vacation or hanging with the family. That is not to say that you should ignore important work-related responsibilities. After your dinner, recital, or whatever other family activity you are partaking in, go take your work calls and put out your fires. However, when you're on family time, be a man, be a dad, be a husband, and be present by staying off the FUCKING phone for that time because the people in your life deserve your attention! UNDERSTAND?!

---

* Cats being afraid of cucumbers (one example of many): https://www.youtube.com/watch?v=cNycdfFEgBc

† Snoop Dogg and Willie Nelson, both musicians, have worked smoking marijuana into their "images," but for 99.999 percent of the population, being stoned all the time is a bad thing.

I remember my phone going off during a date with my then-girlfriend, who is now my wife. She glanced down at the buzzing phone on the table and asked, "Aren't you going to take that?"

I responded, "That's a piece of plastic, and right now I'm talking to a human being. You are more important."

Cell phones and computers are just a means of communicating; they're not a damn leash. She doesn't always appreciate when I apply this rule to her when she calls, but she understands. Also, because she is the most important thing to me, we have a code worked out that tells me when I really need to stop what I'm doing and answer her call.

Your efforts should be focused on building things that matter and surrounding yourself with people who will help you move toward your goals. All other distractions should be removed or regulated to the point that they do NOT AFFECT your work or your goals.

GUIDELINE #4:
EVERY ROADBLOCK CAN HELP YOU.

It is not possible to anticipate every pop-up roadblock life will throw your way. And, in fact, trying to plan for that is completely asinine. If we did that day-to-day, nothing would ever get done. On the other hand, when something goes wrong, don't simply shrug and say, "Shit, life threw me a curveball. Now I can't move forward or accomplish my goals." Instead, evaluate the roadblock and see what it can teach you or which direction it can take you. Brace yourself, Karl Marx, CAPITAL-IZE on it if possible, and change direction if required.

I had a plan, dammit, and I was executing it violently. I had a wife, I had properties, I had a house, I was worth seven figures, the GI Bill was paying for things, and I was moving full steam ahead to be a Gator at University of Florida (UF) like my godmother. I had a 3.56 GPA, I am an Eagle Scout, I am an honorably discharged Marine, I had a clean record apart from a few speeding tickets, and I volunteered in my community. I knew in my soul, beyond a shadow of a friggin' doubt, that I was the best fucking transfer student UF would see that semester! But, as it turned out, I was thrown for a loop. I got divorced, lost half of all my shit, the market crashed, I got into a fistfight with my neighbor, got arrested (over a parking spot), and I was just one class short of UF's transfer requirements. In the face of all these roadblocks (one of which was self-imposed), I sat back, evaluated my situation, learned what I could, and made some new choices but **I never fucking stopped. I kept on going forward.** Don't hate and don't dwell. Instead, learn, adapt, and move forward.

Was I pissed off at my ex-wife for leaving? You're goddamn right I was! Was I pissed off that I was financially set back ten years? Was I fucking angry at the market and how it crashed? Did that shit mess with my ego? YES! Was I pissed off and ashamed that I had added to all this by getting arrested? Abso-fucking-lutely! Was I pissed off that UF would not allow me to take ONE additional class to get into their school? You're damn right I was. Nevertheless, I chose to learn and move forward. I CHOSE not to be angry. I CHOSE to get over it. I CHOSE to IMPROVE! I CHOSE to AT LEAST respect my ex-wife, who is a good woman and who is taking out the trash as a detective in Florida. I chose to ALWAYS learn, ask questions, and know as much as possible about the new choices that life would force me to make. I figured it out, and so can you.

But John, I don't know how to figure it out. Man, you need to pick up your phone, open your laptop, or grab your tablet and hit Google. You can find ANYTHING on Google. (I just Googled "Tyrannosaurus Rex Farts" and literally got 7,560,000 results in 0.36 seconds.) Do your homework and learn about your next step. I also recommend reading Sean Whalen's book, *How to Make Sh*t Happen.* It's a badass read, it's not too long, and he does a great job explaining this guideline in VERY succinct and easy-to-remember terms. There IS NO EXCUSE for not doing your homework or researching to learn from whatever you're facing. Your efforts can, and will, put you on a solid decision-making course to help you handle the sick and twisted shit life throws at you.

You have the same power as Elon Musk or any other rich guy out there. Two men made **all people equal**, and they were Samuel Colt, when he perfected the pistol, and Al Gore when he "invented the internet." With the internet, you have access to every resource you can possibly need to be able to learn from life's curveballs and keep moving forward. (On the other hand, when your eighteen-year-old, 115-pound daughter has a pistol in her hand, she can defend herself against a 250-pound male aggressor. Now that is equality, or at the very least a Marine dad's vision of feminism…but I diverge.)

John! How were you able to capitalize on losing half your properties, losing your money and your things, not being allowed into UF, and being arrested into something positive? Because that very concept sounds like incoherent rhetoric to me.

Well, listen up! I got divorced during my finals of my sophomore year in college. Yeah, my ex-wife called me between finals and literally said, "John, I am moving out now and will be gone before you get home." I had a plan, and I was ready to tackle my finals until life was all like,

HA HA! Try concentrating on your next final now, dude! But NOT being married lead me to spend more time in school, where I met a friend named Mike. We studied hard together and were instant friends. He and I had some good times in Costa Rica together. (He tried to teach me to surf.) As "luck" would have it, he was the first step toward me meeting my new wife, which I'll explain in more detail later.

Next, not being allowed into UF (which I still don't fully understand to this day) opened my options and set me on a path to move to Jacksonville (which, as referenced in *Deadpool* does, in fact, have an awesome TGI Fridays*) where I met my current wife and started a family. All of these negative events led me to call my cousin who had just moved to Jacksonville and I vented to him about not getting into UF.

He said, "John, you should look at UNF. I was standing in line at The Home Depot and overheard two guys talking about how good their construction program is there."

At first, I thought, *What kind of low-down, hoedown, well-them-there-hills school is UNF?* I had never heard of it. I did my homework on the school and eventually drove to Jacksonville to drink beer and shoot potato guns with my cousin. Oh, and I also had an interview at UNF, which turned out to be a very good school (just smallish). The rest is history. I moved to Jacksonville and attended University of North Florida where I earned my BS in building construction, minored in business, and graduated cum laude.

I did not take "no" for an answer…and I was told "no" A LOT! I dug in and worked hard to create my own luck (a.k.a OPPORTUNITY),

---

* I have nothing to do with TGI Fridays, they are not sponsoring me, but it does have decent food, beer and liquor. Just saying Wade Wilson (aka Deadpool) had a point.

I removed distracting shit from my life (and at college there is a half-metric shit-ton of distraction), and I continually sought out new ways to capitalize on the shit life threw—and still throws—at me.

GUIDELINE #5: KNOW WHAT YOU CAN'T CHANGE AND FOCUS ON WHAT YOU CAN CHANGE.

There are many things in life we can't control and other things we can choose to change. When you understand the difference between the two, YOU can make small changes in what YOU do each day to get better and achieve YOUR goals.

The people who are reading this book generally fall into two camps. The first and smallest camp are the people who just simply "get it." Guys like Nikola Tesla, for example. He was out for a walk in 1882 and the Almighty (yes, I believe) flicks him in the forehead and says, "Check this shit out, Nikola." The guy literally stopped walking and sketched the concept of an alternating current electric motor in the dirt. The guy used a fucking patch of dirt to change the world. Other guys like Albert Einstein, Kim Peek (the inspiration for *Rain Man*), Mozart, and Steve Jobs come to mind. These guys just simply wake up, stretch, pour a cup of coffee and say to themselves, *Fuck it. Today I'm gonna make the impossible possible.*

The other, much larger group of people who I call "the rest of us" are the ones this guideline really affects. We are the guys who need to focus on what we can control and then figure out how to make our dreams happen. We wake up and say to ourselves, *Self, I am going to do* _____. We have no dadgum clue really how to get there, but we know there has got to be a way, so we dig in, do our homework, and pursue it.

Guys like Thomas Edison, Henry Ford, Eberhard Anheuser (the German beer guy, gents), Eli Whitney, Carl Jung (the head shrink who set the proverbial bar in his field), and King Camp Gillette are just some who thought to themselves, *There is a better way.* Then they hacked out their own success via trial and error, and created a space for their business, industry, science, or product.

While I was growing up, my family was so poor we could not afford to pay attention! So, I decided to make one small change. I made sure I graduated high school with at least a C average. And just ninety-six hours after I walked across the stage for my high school graduation, I was on Marine Corps Recruit Depot Parris Island, getting "motivated" by drill instructors. At the time, my mother did not want me to join the Marine Corps and she had refused to give me a copy of my birth certificate. I could not change that, so I was forced to go to the state of Florida for a copy of my birth certificate in order to DEP* in my junior year of high school. (See guideline #1 above; "no" never means "no.") I joined my beloved Marine Corps, and my parents did not speak to me for several weeks. I was not able to change the way they felt. But I focused on what I could control and gave it my all in the Marine Corps. I served my country for over six years of my five-year contract because nineteen terrorists decided it would be a good idea to declare war on the US on September 11, 2001. (They were wrong.) I could not control that, either. However, I made sure I was honorably discharged and enrolled in the GI Bill when I got out so I could attend college and keep moving forward.

I enrolled at the local community college, and this time I was determined to be an A-student because I could control how hard I studied.

---

* Delayed Entry Program (DEP): The program allows a high school junior to essentially enlist before he or she graduates high school.

When I tested into school, they were like, "John, you can't read, write, nor add…" (Almost like it had been over six years since I had done anything school-related.) I was remedial as hell AT A COMMUNITY COLLEGE during my first semester. Nevertheless, I graduated from Palm Beach State College with honors and high academic distinction, and I became a member of the National Honor Society. I even earned English Student of the Year in 2007. (Suck on that, remedial John!) Through all of this, one thing I could not control, like I mentioned above, was my then-wife leaving.

Look, I could not control her decision to leave me. (In fact, if you try too hard to control something like that, the law calls this effort "false imprisonment.") When I got married at age twenty-two, I didn't want kids, but by age twenty-six, I did want to start having a family. I tried for a year to not get divorced, and I tried to work things out between us. In the end, we had "irreconcilable differences." Having kids is something a guy can contribute to but can never control; it's that simple. So, the next step was to take a bite out of that shit sandwich life gave me, and so I did.

I got divorced, split half my stuff, was set back ten years financially, and I ended up in Jacksonville, Florida, attending UNF. Something else I could not control was my college buddy, Mike, signing me up for Myspace (before Facebook). He signed me up, uploaded pictures, and built my entire profile. He emailed me the link and password with a caption that read something along the lines of, "Dude the chicks find you on this site; it's great!" He was right, and I ended up meeting Jennifer, my wife and mother of my three kids. This goes back to the adage that you never know what will help you or hurt you, and why you always need to keep evaluating and capitalizing on what life throws at you. Life threw me a divorcee and my buddy threw me a link to a website. I'm better off today than I was back then because I choose to evaluate each thing, determine how it could help me, and move forward. I didn't dwell, and I didn't sink into my head and become lost in the past! I did my homework, made a choice, and moved forward.

When we're faced with something that is out of our control, it's up to us to shift gear, and focus on what we can change. We lick our wounds, drink some beer, and then we make choices that will help us move forward.

Beware, though: Not all choices are good ones. For example, in the middle of everything I mentioned above, I also got into a fistfight with my insane neighbor and ended up getting arrested over a disputed parking spot. The judge tossed the case for a litany of reasons, including a break from a THOUGHTFUL police officer. Look, the point is, we choose to do things. For instance, I chose to get physical with my asshole neighbor and bring him violence he would never forget. I chose to conserve water by smashing his face into the dry spot of the lawn, to water it with his tears and saliva (water conservation is not a laughing matter). I made the decision to do all that. Violence is rarely the answer, and in this case, he stepped up, challenged me, and when he touched me, I reacted. Last I heard, he was a much more polite man than he ever had been. He's stopped yelling at the females in our neighborhood and actually offers to help them every now and again with their trash. It cost me four grand in legal fees, I re-broke two of my fingers punching his head, I ended up with a record, and that damn dry spot on the lawn remained dry. Think *Deadpool*... "STUPID!!! But worth it."

This highlights just how valuable choices can be. What could I have spent that four grand on other than a lawyer? What could have happened to me if I had killed that man? This choice taught me the real-world impact of making choices. Sometimes a guy needs to defend himself, but there is always an impact to the decisions we make. In this case, it was a draw as to it being both good and bad. He learned who the bull in the neighborhood was, and I learned to be more patient with people and just walk away whenever possible. He was an Oompa-Loompa-looking slob who probably couldn't have hurt me physically, and I should have just walked away.

An example of some good choices I made are as follows: I chose to hire on with Barnard Construction after I graduated college. My colleagues and I travel together, build together, and make money together. We use the pronouns "we," "us," and "ours" in emails and conversation, and we spend many holidays together as the "Barnard Family." In a corporate way, Barnard has some of the same attributes as the Marines. I also chose to move to Bozeman, Montana, where it snows in JULY! Now I make great money, I have decent benefits, and I have been able to treat my family better than I was raised by a long shot. And I am NOT done improving. I've been at the company for ten years and IMAGINE THIS, I still have a problem with authority; it's just that now I have learned to focus that energy to be successful. Next on my list is to become a published author and inventor. I am a patent holder as of December 2020, and I'm getting the money together to start two businesses with my wife in 2022.

What I'm getting at is this: Knowing the difference between what you can't control and changing what you can control happens as a series of small steps that build momentum out of the choices you make every day. Each small step builds on the previous steps, all with the explicit goal of creating wealth, being a better man, and providing for yourself and your family.

Be RELENTLESS in your pursuit of money every fucking day. Overcome the words "no," "can't," and "impossible." Work hard to create your own luck and be your own opportunity. Remove distracting, use-less shit from your life, and learn and grow from life's unexpected hic-cups. Finally, know what you can control and what you cannot. Accept that you will fuck it up now and then, and understand there will be times when you will have to change your perspective. Like when I had what Bill Clinton would call "a parking spot-related kinetic mediation session to negotiate and resolve a dispute with my neighbor," or when I found out that "until death do us part" meant five years and bounce, or when my mother refused to provide my birth certificate so I could join the Marine Corp. But you adapt, you change, you **choose to not be angry**, you know what you CAN DO, and you overcome!

To date, I have moved myself and my family from ultra-low-class to upper-middle-class by simply applying these five guidelines. I chose to not care what anyone thinks about me, and I have made the most of every opportunity that came my way. I'm NOT DONE moving up because it's fun, it's exciting, and life is much easier to live when one has MONEY.

I'm sharing these guidelines with you so they can become the corner-stones for you to change your life, too. It's time to put them into prac-tice to get the million dollars out of your head and your ass. Show the world what you think about their fucking canoes!

YOU DETERMINE HOW YOU GET THE MILLION DOLLARS OUT OF YOUR HEAD AND ASS

t is you who decides how to get your million dollars from your head and your ass. That is not a metaphor. You have the potential to create your own success by simply using your head and working your ass off. The five guidelines from the previous chapter will help you get there, but ultimately, it's up to you to determine how you'll make it happen.

The guy who literally personifies using his head and ass is Atiim Kiambu "Tiki" Barber! My two favorite teams are the Miami Dolphins and whoever is playing **any New York team**. I'm not a Giants fan, and I'm not some guy who knows all of Barber's stats, what he did, and how he did it. I don't know his birthday or any of that stuff. (Some guys grew up learning sports. I grew up learning mechanics on the farm.) I can, however, distinguish great game play from good game play, and Barber had great game play.

Tiki Barber was outstanding to watch. He must have had one of the league's highest athletic IQs ever. He would constantly adapt to his opponents, and I swear, he knew what the defense was going to do before they did. Barber retired in 2007 and, as of 2021, he still holds twenty-two of the Giants' franchise records including, but not limited to, longest TD run, most 100-yard games, most 200-yard games, most rushing yards, most total yards, most 1,000-yard seasons, and most fumble recoveries just to highlight a few. He was a VERY physical player. At five feet ten inches, he was not the biggest guy on the field, but he was smarter than most everyone else and he knew how to move the ball and get the damn pigskin to the end zone. He made a lot of very talented defensive linemen look slow, like they should give their paychecks back.

I did some homework on the man to try to understand why a guy in his prime would leave the NFL. I took notice when I read that he quit playing because it was taking a toll on his body, and I dug deeper to find out more about his professional successes.

In the US, we like to pretend we are all created equal, but that is BULLSHIT. We are NOT created equal. And before you go all Jim Acosta on me and start hurling words that end in "-ism" or "-ist", let me explain. (Jim Acosta is a journalist who currently works for CNN. He is the embodiment of what is termed "yellow journalism.") I could train for twelve months straight and NEVER be as fast as Tiki Barber is today, and he has been retired for twelve years. I could train for years and LeBron James will still out-dunk me even if he gave me a giant trampoline advantage. We are NOT all equal, and that IS OKAY! I'd be willing to say I could outperform them both in mechanical troubleshooting because it just comes naturally to me. Similarly, Tiki Barber understood he had God-given talent that most others do not have. He trained hard, honed his skills, and used his physical advantage in his youth. Later, he left the sport when he was literally at the top of his game. After his NFL career where he used his physical strength to make a great living, Tiki transitioned to broadcasting where he used his head to take the next step in his success.

Barber majored in business at the University of Virginia, has co-authored more than ten books, and is more articulate than almost any other sports correspondent in the business. Beyond all that, Barber has multiple business ventures and has appeared on multiple TV shows and on Broadway.

I came to admire his professional prowess. I thought, *Here is a guy who decided to start using the six inches between his ears to make a good living.* As it turns out, he was doing that from **day fucking one.** And THAT is exactly what I had in mind when I got out of the Marines to pursue a college degree. It made sense to me. I used my strength to make money when I was in the Marines and then I used my head to make money after I went to school.

Tiki Barber took full advantage of the body he was BORN WITH and used it to earn money and build a good life. As he got older, he transitioned using his God-given brains to continue to build his empire. This took NOTHING away from anyone else in the process. He had no type of privilege, his masculinity is not toxic, and he had no advantages. In fact, he was on the small side for the NFL, and yet he still KILLED IT on the field and off the field. He didn't let "no" stop him, he made his own opportunity, he kept his eye on the ball, he knew what he could do and what he couldn't do, and he adapted along the way. He never appeared to care what others thought about him, and he made his career on his own. He literally used his ass when he was younger and then his HEAD when he got older to keep making money and further his domain.

In this world, you are NOT climbing up to get to the top of one thing or another. You are, in fact, climbing a metaphorical mountain. But it's not just ONE mountain; it's an entire chain of mountains. Only after we reach the top of one mountain can we see the next one. It may be higher or it may be lower than the one we just climbed. (We will discuss this concept in more detail in a later chapter.)

I got out of the Marines, where I definitely used my ass to make money, and segued into college where I used my head to earn a BS in Building Construction. I was an A-student and graduated cum laude. Then I took a job at a construction company, and when I interned, I was in charge of water control (a.k.a the "pump bitch") and JUST LIKE THAT I was back to using my back to make money.

Then I ended up in the home office where I arrived an honorably discharged Marine who had graduated in the top of his class, was thirty-one years old, and guess what? They handed me a fucking shovel and told me to go shovel the snow off the sidewalks. My "office" (like many others' at the time) was in an overflow closet next to the bathroom. Here I was thinking I was "moving up" and they handed me a shovel and stuck me in a closet. I was using a combination of my head and ass to make money.

From there, I have been given several crews and worked them safely and productively to make money and do things for our organization that have never been attempted before at the scale we have done them. I got to lead my two teams and use my head to make money.

THERE IS NO SUCH THING AS PRIVILEGE

The word "privilege" is defined by *Merriam-Webster's Dictionary* as, "a right or immunity granted as a peculiar benefit, advantage, or favor: especially: such a right or immunity attached specifically to a position or an office." This definition has changed in recent years. Today, privilege is used as a way to disparage success and reinforce laziness, the status quo, and apathy!

Privilege is the invention of a bunch of people who are looking to justify their own ineptitude and slothfulness. There are so many types of privilege today; It's hard to keep track:

- Ability: Being able-bodied

- Economic: Having doors open for you because of your financial resources

- Education: Having access to good education

- Gender: In today's society, being a male is considered a privilege

- Race: Being white, apparently, holds some sort of advantage over people of color

And the list goes ON and ON.

But these so-called privileges ignore the complexities and specifics of each person's situation that have led them to success. For example, in school we dissect a situation, study it until it is exhausted, and then we believe we understand what happened based on the principle of cause and effect. But these lessons are almost ALWAYS STATIC! There is VERY little that is studied in school within dynamic or changing circumstances. Think of school as if it were a laboratory. In the lab, everything is controlled. In fact, there is a specific group in every experiment called the "control group," for fuck's sake.

Controls are defined as variables that are kept the same throughout the experiment because they are not of primary concern in the experimental outcome. Any change in a control variable in an experiment would **invalidate the correlation of dependent variables (DV) to the independent variable (IV), thus skewing the results.** *But John, what the fuck does that even mean?* It means that if you change one little thing in the experiment, the entire outcome changes. (Think *The Butterfly Effect* starring Ashton Kutcher.)

It is easy to compare a trust-fund baby who went to college, landed a good job, and became rich versus a poor inner-city kid who is predestined to join a gang, shoot up a convenience store, and land in prison. If you keep the controls of each situation the same, that comparison works. So, if the rich trust-fund baby keeps his nose clean and the poor kid doesn't know right from wrong, the experiment proves that rich trust-fund babies do better than poor inner-city kids, right? Then how did Ben Carson go from the inner city to become the Secretary of Housing and Urban Development for the President of the United States? Oh, and that was **after he became a neurosurgeon!** (Yeah, a fucking brain surgeon, and a badass one who saved kids' lives and shit.) And then how did Bernie Madoff go from being SUPER FUCKING rich to being a convicted felon? (I'm not sure that Bernie will do all that well in prison.)

It's also easy to assume that an amputee has a disadvantage over a guy who is able-bodied. Yet I would pay to watch someone tell combat-wounded Marine Veteran Jose Luis Sanchez that he is disadvantaged and cannot do something a guy with two legs can do. (Jose would chase him down, tackle him, and beat the shit out of him with his prosthetic leg, just to prove a point.)

In reality, when people say someone has some sort of privilege or advantage that accounts for their success, they are only speaking academically. (They have ALSO never paid attention to **any of the *Jurassic Park* movies**! What happens when you change **one single control**? In *Jurassic Park* terms, "nature finds a way." Just ask Jeff Goldblum; he'll unbutton his shirt and tell you all about it.) When you release the controls and the experiment becomes dynamic—or exposed to real life—reality will roundhouse-kick "privilege" right in its fucking mouth, just as it should do.

It DOES NOT matter where you came from, what you look like, how many limbs you have, whether you like to date the opposite sex or the same sex, or what god you choose to worship. If you WORK HARD and follow the five guidelines listed in chapter one, you **will be as successful as you want to be**! That's just a fact. **This is America!** The trust-fund baby has just as much opportunity to succeed as he does of becoming a meth-head who steals his mom's shit for dope. And the inner-city kid can outperform his so called "privileged" counterparts by simply reaching for his goals, following the five guidelines, and working harder than his competition.

A simple example of this is as follows: An elementary school teacher was trying to show her class how "privilege" works. She had all the kids roll a piece of paper into a ball. Then she placed a trash can in the front of the classroom. Next, she had the kids in the first row of desks stand up and shoot their paper balls into the trash can like a basketball. Then the next row stood up and airmailed their paper balls into the trash can. This process continued until the fourth row of kids took their turn. Each time a row did this, she would count how many students made their paper ball into the trash can. The first row of kids, who were closest to the can, sunk 100 percent of their paper balls; the second row had a 75 percent success rate; the third row had a 50 percent success rate; and the fourth row had a dismal 10 percent success rate. This experiment showed that if you were closer to the trash can you had a better chance of making it in. In other words, the first row was "privileged" to be closer to the trash can, just as some of us start out life with a better chance of success than others. (But remember, this is ONLY a correlation.)

But wait! Little Timmy in row four was a bit of a clown and had a splash of ADD. He wanted to make the basket, so he ran up to the trash can, passed the paper ball between his legs like LeBron James, stuck his tongue out like Michael Jordan, jumped, and slam-dunked his ball into the trash can, yelling, "You just got schooled!" as the trash can fell over, spilling out all the trash. Apart from earning a detention, what just happened to Timmy? **He did the work!** He didn't know he was disadvantaged. He took the time to evaluate the situation and he knew that, in order to make the basket, he had to get closer to it, so he did just that. He changed the equation! **He changed the control**, and in doing so, **he fucking invalidated the damn correlation to the dependent variables.**

The simple fact is that "privilege" as it is defined today, is based solely on correlation…and correlation can be one big pile of crap. Did you know that in Chicago there is a correlation between murders and sales of ice cream? It's true. When ice cream sales spike, murders spike, too! That's because in the winter no one wants to go outside, so murders go down. It's also too damn cold to want to eat ice cream. There is a correlation, **but no causation!** People are not getting all hopped-up on Nutty Buddys, then grabbing their 9mm and shooting motherfuckers. The same goes for privilege. There is an absolute correlation between being closer to a trash can and successfully sinking your paper ball, but that doesn't mean a kid from the back row cannot slam-dunk his in the can. ANYONE—and I mean ANYONE—can take the time to get closer to the trash can and make a slam-dunk if they only do the work.

Another element of this argument is adversity, which is thought to be the reason why people without "privilege" are less likely to be successful. In truth, adversity is the key to success. Over the course of our history, we have thrived on adversity. Some of our greatest advances have come from times of war, famine, and great hardship. One need look no further than WWII to see that this is true. The guided torpedo and the proximity fuze for artillery shells were both developed to support our war effort during WWII. If we had failed to develop these items, the casualties for our men would have been even higher than they were, and we could have lost the war (and this book would be written in German or Japanese…if it would have been allowed at all).

Idle time spent hanging out at the BBQ pit drinking beer with friends and contemplating all our fucking privilege won't spark innovation. It takes hardship and difficulty to bring things to a high point of development. This concept has been proven over and over again. In fact, it is so popular that it has given rise to the cliché, "Idle hands are the devil's play toy." Let a guy go without anything constructive to work toward and he will find something stupid to do. Just look at the character

Russell Casse from the movie *Independence Day* to see a gleaming example of this. He goes from a drunk fuck-up to a hero because he has something constructive to do in the face of adversity.

A great example of overcoming adversity can be found in my personal friend, Dave Dick. Dave owns a multimillion-dollar construction company and has overcome a fuck-load of personal and economic adversity to make his success. After a failed back surgery, Dave was prescribed several prescriptions of morphine, oxycodone, and Roxicodone, which paved the way to an addiction. He would go through a week's worth of his prescription in just three days. At one point, Dave purchased 100 pills from his dealer and in a one-day period, from 10 a.m. to 5 p.m., he took 67 pills, had a car accident, and collapsed in his house. His wife found him on the floor. By his own admission, Dave was prescribed heavy doses of opioids, but it was **his choice to abuse them**. Dave informed me that he barely remembers the month of October 2016, and that his employees had to take the reins and steer the company to keep it afloat. Dave spent $26,000 on online auctions for a pickup truck, a heavy-haul trailer, and a Hummer H and didn't remember it until he was sober. (Sober Dave was able to turn a profit on those purchases.)

Dave decided to tackle his addiction after his wife gave him an ultimatum to get help or get out. This was a huge wake-up call for him as it meant the potential loss of his family and his business. Dave went to the same doctor who first prescribed him the drugs and asked for help. He was put on Suboxone, which is an opioid blocker, and it changed his life forever. Five days later, Dave took his last opioid-based pill to date.

Dave's example is an embodiment of hitting **rock fucking bottom** because of adversity, hardship, and suffering. Today, he is sober and has used his experience to help others overcome their addictions. He wore his tribulation on his sleeve and showed others who were addicts how hard work and dedication can change your life. He literally showed them how to change. Be ashamed and you will fail and never overcome your adversity, be it drug addiction or being poor.

When Dave realized he could lose everything because of his addiction, that adversity actually opened a door that pushed him to rebuild his life bigger and better than before. Moreover, his business is healthier now than it ever was. Privilege is synonymous with apathy and slothfulness, and **it fucking closes doors; it sure as shit does NOT open them.**

Struggle, strife, hardship, discipline, and what I like to call "proper direction of anger" (PDA) work to create success. *But wait, John, anger is a blocked wish* and clouds the mind.* Just hold it right there with the psychobabble. You're talking about blind rage or hatred. But well-placed, properly directed anger is a very powerful tool. To quote Clint Eastwood from *The Outlaw Josey Wales*, "…when things look bad and it looks like you're not gonna make it, then you gotta get mean. I mean plumb, mad-dog mean. 'Cause if you lose your head and you give up, then you neither live nor win…" In Marines terms, PDA is the relentless pursuit of a goal, an unwillingness to retreat, and a CONSTANT evolution of one's perspective in order to overcome whatever life throws at you.

We all need a challenge, a goal, or a hardship to push us to "level up" in society. To make more money, you first need to feel uncomfortable with the status quo. You do NOT need comfort or "privilege." Privilege as a means to get further in one's position in life is a myth. It's like Sasquatch, **it does not fucking exist.**

---

* "Anger is a Blocked Wish," *Analyze This.* https://www.youtube.com/watch?v=p1uQ3SQEPko

YOU CATCH MORE FLIES WITH BULLSHIT THAN YOU DO WITH HONEY: THE KEY TO BUILDING RELATIONSHIPS AND NETWORKING

entlemen, this is the single biggest thing you can do to better your situation. Build relationships at home, with your girlfriend or your wife (this will not work if you have a wife AND a girlfriend), with your kids, your neighbors, your business partners, the police, the firefighters, and everyone else not listed here. This takes a great deal of consideration and time, but not too much work to do.

By creating connections, you will attract more people into your network and expand your opportunities both personally and professionally. For example, we have a great broker named Ben who handles my family's estate. He is average height and pasty white, with fingernails chewed down to the cuticle and a waistline that exceeded the maximum weight limit on his belt a long time ago. He wears what I would call "birth control glasses" because when you wear them no chick will ever want to date you, let alone take you to bed.

One day, I met his wife, who is an absolute knockout and head-turner. She is five feet seven inches, 120 pounds soaking wet, with long legs, a tight body, great complexion, beautiful eyes, a splash of freckles, a great smile, and long flowing dark blonde locks. I remember thinking she was a trophy wife; that seemed to be the only way he could have landed a gal like that.

After spending time with Ben and watching him work, I came to find that he is confident and considerate in pretty much everything he does. This applies to his personal AND professional relationships. He is brilliant and can work through most things quickly, easily, correctly, and smoothly. A pasty-white fat guy with all the curb appeal of a 1970 Ford Pinto can land a great-looking gal and start a beautiful family because he took the time to build the relationship and be considerate.

The same goes for professional success. If you want to pull that million dollars out of your ass, you have got to build relationships and take the time to get to know the guys you're dealing with. Do this right and the sky is the limit. (Dammit, Elon Musk, the launch of your BFR strikes again because the sky is no longer the limit, is it?) Do this right and there is no limit to how far you can go. (That doesn't exactly roll off the tongue there, Elon.)

There's an old adage that goes, "You catch more flies with honey than you will with vinegar," meaning it's best to be nice to people because they will be nice to you in return, and you will get more out of them. But that adage is total bullshit. If you want to catch flies, you use bullshit. Not literal bullshit (although that is where flies typically hang out), but you bullshit (talk and chitchat) with people for a little while about stuff that is NOT business-related. Take the time to get to know the person on the other side of the deal you are trying to make. Get a bit personal with them and understand what makes them tick. You don't have to play twenty questions; just work in a comment like, "I'm having lunch with my wife," or "I can't believe this weather we are having." These comments are simple and benign, but they WILL segue to things you have in common and subjects you can agree on. These conversation-openers also help you gauge what you can get away with, or what you can say and what you should not say during the negotiation process. Simply put, you become a human being to them, rather than just a contract or cooperation.

For example (and stay with me here because this book is NOT political, although politics earned Barnard Construction over $40,000 in pure profit last year), I was trying to make a contract that was worth over $500,000 to buy bolts from a longtime supplier (literally tons of bolts which took three semitrailers to deliver). We negotiated for several months to try to reach an amicable accord. During this time, I learned he worked and lived in California and hated the high taxes he had to pay. I also learned that he was business savvy, he cared about the end user and the product he was selling, and he wanted to build and maintain relationships for the future. I found out he was married and had many of the same views about raising a family as I did. We also knew some of the same people in the industry. By gauging his language, I also determined that he leaned toward the right, even though I never asked him his political affiliation.

Long story short, our contracts have very strict performance requirements. If a supplier fails to provide us with quality materials, we will assemble a gaggle of lawyers and come after them like a fucking rabid bulldog. Needless to say, he wanted to amend this part of the contract which, at my level, I was not permitted to do. Instead, I responded with, "You are not going into this with the intention to fail, are you? We will not come after you if you provide the quality that I know you can deliver."

Now, at that time, Brett Kavanaugh had just been selected by President Donald Trump to become an Associate Justice of the Supreme Court. Kavanaugh was being dragged through the swamp that is Washington DC when Christine Blasey Ford made a sexual assault claim against him. Kavanaugh denied the claim, but at the time the headlines all read "Believe Ford" and "#BelieveWomen," etc.

So, naturally, after I told the bolt supplier if he provided a quality product we would not come after him, he fired back with, "Oh, okay Professor Ford, I guess I am just supposed to believe everything you say, right?!"

This was his way of showing his concern that I can "say" we will not come after him, but the contract would still allow for it.

I replied with, "No, I'm more like Kavanaugh and I say what I mean and do what I say."

We both chuckled for a second, and **the tone of the argument was instantly lowered**.

Because he and I took the time to get to know one another, neither of us were offended (and the subject of politics was now on the table to be brought into conversation). Those comments also led me to pivot and capitalize on another political hot-button issue at the time: the China-US trade war. President Trump was renegotiating steel tariffs with China in an effort to get them to buy more US-produced goods, and China just happened to be where our bolts would be produced.

So, after we stopped chuckling about the Ford-Kavanaugh ribbing, I asked him, "Would an up-front payment allow you to secure your materials to make our bolts now and avoid potential tariffs?"

He said, "Yes it would."

So, I tossed him an option where we would give him $100,000 up front with proof of material purchase if he dropped the overall contract value by $40,000. AND HE BIT! He signed the contract the next day, and two months of negotiation was over; I had successfully negotiated the deal.

Yeah, we bullshitted for a good long while, but in the meantime, we were learning each other's sense of humor and ended up using absurd politics as a means of getting the contract to an amicable point. At the end of the day, he felt comfortable he would not get screwed if a tariff was enacted and my company saved a great deal of money in the process. I cannot wait until the next time I have to order something big from him. He knows my name, what I do, and what I can provide for him, and vice versa. Just like that, we networked. Ha! They don't teach you that in school!

The goal is to build the relationship to make money. This means learning what makes the other person tick. How you get there is up to you, but this does NOT mean you should bulldoze and fuck the other guy over or force them to adopt your points of view.

It does not matter whether you want the next business deal, the hot chick at the end of the bar, or a marriage that's all fifty-shades hot. It ALL requires relationship development. **Say what you mean, and then do what you say.** Take the TIME to get to know the person across from you. Learn what they like and where you both have common interests. Be natural about it; skip the twenty questions and just let the other person talk. And be CONSIDERATE! For example, if you hear them mention church, avoid using the word "goddammit" in your vernacular. Or, if you hear them mention San Francisco or Seattle, mention how great the food or art is there or mention the local football team. This makes them feel heard and will create COMMON GROUND so you can build on the relationship.

Without question, there will be some people who are incredibly bat-shit crazy to deal with. In those instances, you should not just walk away, but rather RUN away. For example, think of all the people who had to work with Harvey Weinstein, Matt Lauer, Bill O'Reilly, and Kevin Spacey. Those guys are crazy! Professionally, you will come across some people who just do not consider the other party, are strictly out for themselves, and have no clue how to network. Nevertheless, those instances are rare because those people do not last long, and after word gets out no one wants to deal with them.

With those exceptions aside, it's simple shit that seals the deals! You would not walk up to someone you are attracted to and start talking to them about religion straightaway. Instead, you would introduce yourself first and comment about something she is doing or wearing, or you would mention the mutual friend you both share. The same is true professionally. By doing this one simple thing, doors will open that you never knew were there. You will ALWAYS catch more flies with bullshit than you will with honey.

The guidelines are the same for personal and professional relationship development with VERY little exception:

Are you attracted to her?

Approach her with confidence and good posture. Communicate that you have your stuff together (and lose the fucking man-bun if you have one).

Get to know her. Ask her what she is drinking, or if she is there alone or with friends.

Invite her out to a public place such as a club, a restaurant, or another quieter bar.

Stop staring at her and LISTEN to the words coming out of her mouth. Then remember what she says and reply to those comments.

Relate to her when you can, and when you can't relate, be sympathetic to her situation. **Do not problem solve.** Just listen and gauge whether you're a good fit together. Find out where she is going in life and evaluate whether your paths will overlap enough for a second date. **Again, do not ask** a ton of questions. She will tell you everything you need to know if you just LISTEN.

When she asks you a question, keep your answer succinct and direct. Don't try and "church up" what you have done or where you have been because that shit will bite you in the ass, and you will lose her trust and the relationship. Be honest, don't brag, and then take it from there.

Are they suited to complete the job at hand? Can they get the job done on a technical and physical level?

Approach them with confidence and good posture. Show them that what you bring to the table is professional and top shelf, and that you will make them money. (Again, lose the fucking man-bun if you have one!)

Get to know the team you hope to work with. Find out where their home office is located and Google the address so you can talk about their local attractions, sports team, etc. Find common ground. Invite them out to what we in construction call a "job walk." Get to know the lay of the land with them so you can speak on common, neutral ground.

LISTEN to what they are saying. Their comments to small things will tell you what they are thinking and where they are going in the big picture. Then remember what they say and gauge your responses accordingly.

Relate to them and give examples of how you overcame similar circumstances, but do not give away anything proprietary. Where you cannot be sympathetic to their situations, lean in and ask how they overcame them.

Answer their questions succinctly and directly. Don't try and "oversell" what you can offer because that shit will bite you in the end, and you will lose their confidence and their business.

CHOOSE YOUR CLAN

Ask yourself where you want to be in life. Do you want to be a mid-level employee? Do you want to be a CEO? Do you want to run your own business? Do you want to be a better husband, lover, and friend to your wife or girlfriend? Do you want to learn a new hobby, like surfing or marksmanship? Or do you want to be a do-nothing bum? Whatever you aspire to be, hang out with those people. To be greater, surround yourself with people who strive to be better. If you associate with people who are content with where they are, that is exactly where you will stay: right where you (and they) are. But if you want to climb up, hang out with the people you want to become. YOU are the average of the five people you spend the most time with. You will pick up their habits, good and bad. You will pick up **all their habits**, be them smoking, eating, work ethic, relationship status, or business prowess. So, choose those five people wisely. See guideline #3 in chapter one.

Choosing your clan will probably lead to some of the most painful choices you'll ever make. You may have some people in your life right now who are weighing you down more than the anchors on the fucking USS Missouri. You have been loyal to them for years and you consider them dear friends, but they are not supporting you, they don't root for you to win, and they don't make you better. And if you continue to associate with them, you will never get better.

"Great spirits have always encountered opposition from mediocre minds. The mediocre mind is incapable of understanding the man who refuses to bow blindly to conventional prejudices and chooses instead to express his opinions courageously and honestly."

—ALBERT EINSTEIN

Once you start surrounding yourself with successful people, you will naturally be drawn away from your old anchors. While these "friends" are worried about the next Razor or new gadget they can buy, you will be focusing on growing yourself through coaching, buying assets, or investing wisely. You will be hanging out with business owners, entrepreneurs, and producers. Thus, you will not have time to hang out with people who were keeping you small, and that is a good thing.

Now, you don't have to just say "fuck off" and never talk to your old friends. That would be juvenile and would only serve to inflate your own ego. Instead, be truthful with them. Explain that your goals necessitate associating with the guy who owns four bars in town, or runs two car dealerships, or owns a construction company. If they are real friends, they will support you! Hell, they might even ask if they can hang out with those guys, too. The people you do and don't want around you will sort themselves out very quickly. The ones who say, "Oh, you're just brown nosing," or "You're just going to ride his coattails," are the ones you do not need in your life. Anyone who belittles you or tries to dissuade you from bettering yourself is not a friend; they are just an anchor and need to be let go.

My Italian Great Grandma, Roselia Fazzio, knew this concept well and would say, *"La persona che vive con gli storpi imparerà presto a zoppicare,"* which means, "The person who lives with cripples will soon learn to limp." In other words, choose your clan wisely because you WILL take on the traits of those around you, both good and bad.

When John F. Kennedy instructed our nation to put a man on the moon by the end of 1969, did NASA hire nine A-level aerospace engineers and one D-level aerospace engineer? After learning we were in an atomic weapons race with Nazi Germany, did Roosevelt look up and say, "Get me nine of the best physicists you can find, and throw in one physicist who graduated from Billy-Bob's University so he can pick up good habits"? No, they did not. The best and the brightest were all put into a room, handed a problem, and told to solve it.

Be that picky about choosing your own clan. CHOOSE to be the best at what you do. CHOOSE to hang around people who will make you work harder and make you think smarter. CHOOSE to keep your sights high, take on work that challenges you, and **keep moving forward**.

Surround yourself with people you can learn from so that you ALWAYS strive to understand better and know more. ALWAYS! At some point, tying your shoes was hard, but you didn't quit learning once you mastered that one skill. You didn't just shrug and say, "Well, I'm good now. I got that shoe-tying shit down, so I'll never learn anything new from here on out." NO! You kept moving forward and kept looking for the next hard thing to do. And the single greatest way to skyrocket your learning is by spending time with people who have similar goals or who have already achieved the success you are working toward. Never stop asking questions and never stop learning. Life would be fucking BORING if you knew all the answers. Think about that for a second. You would end up like Bill Murray in *Groundhog Day*. It would suck. You need to decide to change, and just like Bill Murray, only then will you move forward.

But John, some people don't like it when I ask questions and they get defensive. Yeah, that will happen sometimes. When you start asking questions, you WILL come across as intimidating and that can scare some people. But you will overcome that quickly because your work will speak for itself and those who are intimidated by you will expose themselves for what they are. You will then have to figure out how to keep those people in the loop while also shifting your focus to other, more helpful people. It's a fine line sometimes.

Choosing your clan means separating from those who would hold you down and those who are naysayers. This even sometimes applies to family members. That doesn't mean you simply drop your family, but you do not want to waste your time talking to them about business if they just don't get it. And as you become more successful, some family members will take note and may think that you owe them something, or they will comment about your success but won't recognize any of the hard work it took for you to get there. Blood IS thicker than water, and family should come first, but take notice of those family members who don't support your success. They may have to be recategorized as being in the loop, but not in your clan.

Just as some of your family may not acknowledge and support your success, you will come across doubters and critics in your friendships and in your professional life, too. I have been told on many occasions, "John, it must be easy for you because _____" (fill in the blank with whatever perceived advantages come to mind). Never mind the weeks of hard work, completed projects, hours of studying, or the tools that were used to assist me on my journey. Many will not see all that has gone into your achievements, and some people just don't want you to succeed. I can hear it now: *That is cynical, John, and a terrible outlook to have.* Many people **don't want you to succeed** because they don't want their own laziness or failures to be brought into sharp-relief* by comparison. The only thing you can do to overcome that is to **choose your clan**! Get away from those who want to see you fail and start hanging around those who want to see you hit the ball out of the park. That goes for your friends, your family, your partner, your coworkers, your acquaintances, and anyone else in your life. Choose your clan wisely and distance yourself from those who will hold you back, like Khaleesi did in *Game of Thrones* (umm, for the most part).

If you want to start a business, make friends with other entrepreneurs and business owners, or join a local club about the type of business you want to start. Chat online with other successful people. Get a mentor in your desired field and follow their lead; do what they do. I'll say it again, **do what they do**! Warren Buffett once said, "Someone's sitting in the shade today because someone planted a tree a long time ago." Use the tools and resources that have been provided for you by others and do your work to the best of your ability. See what makes others successful in their field and emulate those traits.

For example, if you're working at a restaurant and want to own one yourself someday, start hanging out with the owner. Don't go smoke weed in the parking lot with the other servers. Learn how the owner runs his business—pay attention to how the food is rotated, how bills are managed, and how the crews are led (remember, you MANAGE things and you LEAD people). Do you think the guy who owns the restaurant hangs out with employees or with other business owners? He's definitely hanging with other owners! So, by proximity, if you put yourself into his sphere of influence, you will be exposed to other

---

* Sharp relief: An art expression. A relief sculpture can be carved into a wall or flat piece of stone. Older weathered sculptures are rounded and harder to see because they are not defined. When something is in "sharp relief," it's easily seen.

successful people who have overcome challenges you will face in the future.

Choosing your clan is simple enough if you can remove emotion when distancing yourself from those who are holding you back. BE POLITE to those you have to go around in order to be successful, and simply gauge what you say to them and how much time you spend with them.

Finally, internalize this concept by never stopping to strive to improve yourself. Be the person other guys will want to choose for their clan! Get up every day and ask yourself how you can be a better husband, a better father, a better employee, and a better man. Even when you do something good, evaluate it for places of improvement.

WORK, LEARN, LEAD, REPEAT!

Work. We all have to do it, but we don't necessarily have to do it for someone else, we don't have to do it for money, and work doesn't have to be physical.

No matter what job you're doing, work is a manifestation of purpose, and we all require purpose. Show me a person without purpose who is happy. I've never met one, I've never heard of one, and I've never read about one in history.

Now, purpose does not automatically make you happy, but it is a key component of who we are as human beings. (Ask any young Marine cleaning the head* on a Thursday. They have purpose, but they more often than not aren't happy with that purpose.) German philosopher Friedrich Nietzsche once said, "Those who have a 'why' to live, can bear almost any 'how'."

I don't know if it's divine, evolutionary, or just some random requirement the cosmos gave us, but having purpose is undoubtedly necessary, and the only way to check that box is with work.

---

* "Head" is a nautical term for the restroom.

You can work forever making big rocks into little rocks with a screw-driver if enough time is allotted, but that would get boring. The same goes for your work, too. So how do you get better at work? You learn. You watch someone else using a pickax (or preferably explosives) and you repeat what you see them doing. Learning is tied to purpose. Shit, learning can BE a purpose.

After you work and have learned, it is time to lead. I can't emphasize this enough: Managing is NOT leading. We are more valuable collectively when we teach others how to do work better. Managing is reserved for things that cannot think for themselves. You manage equipment, budgets, and diets. But if you manage people, you stifle their creativity and destroy their purpose. Leadership, on the other hand, is magnified by the number of people we can successfully lead. For example, if you teach ten people how to be 10 percent more efficient, you've effectively doubled the effectiveness of that group of people.

Leadership is single-handedly one of the hardest things I have ever had to execute. It's also something that doesn't produce immediate results. Sometimes your leadership can take twenty years to show the fruits of your labor. But positively affecting those around you is a reward like no other.

The second hardest part is to repeat the process again and again. Reaching a place of leadership can feel like the pinnacle, but that will last just long enough for you to realize that the mountain you've crested isn't actually the tallest in the range. Now you have to repeat. You have to work again, but this time the work revolves around leadership. You work at making everyone around you better, all while working at making yourself better, too. When you've learned to do that, you will become a leader of leaders. As you repeat this process, you'll see that you are not actually climbing up, you're moving forward. And that process of moving forward has ups and downs. You may think you are climbing one mountain when in reality you're traversing a mountain range. I believe we have so many bad leaders in the world because of this.

Too often, people reach one peak and just stop. They don't grow, and they don't keep moving. And the next peak is not always higher than the last one reached. Some are lower, less glamorous, and with fewer rewards, so they lie to themselves and say they've achieved enough. Even the lower peaks have value. In fact, many times they have more value than the higher ones but may not look as sexy. For example, driving an Indy car IS sexier than being they guy who fuels it at a pit stop, but that $15 million car will not move an inch without fuel! I bet supermodel Adriana Lima would pose with the car and driver, but not with the gallon of fuel. (Can you blame her?)

These concepts are challenging to understand and even more difficult to execute. The problems surrounding a manager are typically thought to be the fault of someone else and are someone else's responsibility to fix. But the problems surrounding a leader are the fault of the leader, and those problems are the leader's responsibility to fix. Jocko Willink says it best in his book, *Extreme Ownership* (if you have not read this book, stop and order it NOW), "There are no bad teams, only bad leaders." If you are leading a team that is having shitty results, look squarely at yourself. Does your team suck? Then you better go look in the mirror.

Leadership is not only important in our jobs or businesses, but it also shows up in our relationships, our world view, and our interactions with everyone around us. At some point, we will all encounter someone who we try to help become more successful. Maybe it is a brother-in-law who lost his job, a homeless person you give money to on the street, or a friend who wants to buy a toy rather than investing in their future. You give your brother-in-law a room in your house. You hand a $10 bill to the homeless person. You try to convince your friend to do something different. But not one of these "fixes" will help the other person on a long-term basis. Your brother-in-law will get comfortable and will come to expect a place to live. The homeless person will either be a scammer or will squander the money. And your friend will resent your efforts, feel judged, and will probably make the purchase anyway.

This brings us to the parable of the lighthouse and the tugboat. Both guide ships to safety, but their methods are markedly different.*

The tugboat hooks onto the ship, pulling and pushing, and fighting against the mass of the boat. If the boat overpowers the tugboat, it can potentially crash the tugboat. Or if the ship sinks, it can pull the tugboat down with it.

The lighthouse, on the other hand, is fixed in place. It does not move, nor does it directly affect the ship. It just says, "Here I am, I'm experienced, I know where the rocks are, take it or leave it, dipshit." The lighthouse leaves the choice up to the ship. The ship can choose to ignore the beacon and crash, or follow the lighthouse's advice and make it into the harbor safely. The lighthouse also doesn't go looking for ships to save; it just does its thing and shines a light for those ships willing to be helped.

---

* Sean Whalen's book, *How to Make Sh✱t Happen*, goes deeper into the lighthouse parable.

Be the lighthouse and show people what being a good leader does for you and those around you. Work your ass off, learn every chance you get, lead people to make them better, and then repeat the whole process over again. If the people around you fall down, don't pick them up. Instead, show them how to climb back up, outflank the problem they are facing, and overcome it themselves.

Look, when someone is young, they are generally more ignorant to how things work. We don't just wake up and suddenly understand how business works or how the day-to-day activities work. This is why most young workers are the doers, not the planners or leaders. Over time, by putting in the work and learning the ropes, those doers become leaders. This same concept is all around us, we just haven't recognized it. Ask yourself why *Star Wars*, *Deadpool*, *The 13ᵗʰ Warrior*, *Tremors*, *Harry Potter*, *Jaws*, *Avengers*, *Iron Man*, *Game of Thrones*, and even *Sharknado* were such successful movies. What do they all have in common? They all have a character that starts out not knowing what to do with their situation, and over the course of the movie they learn the necessary skills, adapt to their skill set, and become solid at what they do. Finally, they move on to rise as a LEADER and command what they know so they can lead others in doing the same task. It's a simple formula to make millions!

When I joined the Marines, I graduated boot camp as a basically trained Marine, then went to A-school and learned how to take apart helicopters, repair them, and put them back together again. I did that for about three years, during which time I became quite knowledgeable and then began to lead other Marines in the same tasks.

Another earlier example of this concept occurred during high school when I was working at Burger King. I was sixteen years old at the time and was just making money to take my girlfriend out to the movies and put gasoline in my car. I had been told to give out exactly three napkins and two ketchup packets with every meal. If the customer asked for more, I was instructed to give them however many they wanted. I was also told to upsell things like tomatoes and cheese (it was 15 cents for cheese and 5 cents to add tomatoes to a sandwich). I did this because I was asked to by my boss, and I learned early on to make the people who control your food and your paychecks happy or things can get a bit messy (full pun intended). Anyhow, after about six months of doing this, I proved to have a knack for upselling and ended up with the highest ticket average of our store, which was my goal (a ticket average is the average price of all your sales for the day). This got the attention of the higher-ups and they decided to send me, at age sixteen, to Burger King College, which was a training course that lasted about three days.

It was there that I learned why I was doing all that packet-counting and upselling. For example, I learned that a ketchup packet costs one-tenth of a cent to make. That seems like nothing, but if you give out one additional packet per customer at your store and you have 1,000 customers per day, that's $1 lost per day. That's $7 lost per week, $28 a month, and $365 lost per year. Do that at all 17,796 locations and that's a loss of $6,495,540 per year because of a damn ketchup packet. That should piss you off a little when you think about the gas stations that are charging you .009 cents per gallon and rounding up each gallon every-fucking-time!

Before I attended the course, I had been doing the work, taking the orders, ringing them up, and asking the right questions, but I didn't know WHY. I had to take that next step to learn why those details mattered. After that course, my perspective changed a little. I understood why I was doing what I was being asked to do, and I began to teach others how to do it. And, more importantly, I could explain to them **why the fuck it mattered**, and I was able to get buy-in from my team as early as possible. Basically, I became the lighthouse on that proverbial rock. Another year later, they offered me a management position after I completed my senior year of high school. I turned them down because I wanted to be a US Marine and, quite frankly, I thought I would have better luck with the opposite sex while wearing my Marine Corps uniform than I would while wearing a Burger King uniform. (I was right, just ask any woman.)

It doesn't matter if you are a drive-through teller at Burger King, a race car driver, a doctor, a professional athlete, a garbage truck driver, a mechanic, or a Marine. When you are young or starting a new career, you do the work, you learn as much as you possibly can, and as you get older, you continue to better understand the situation so you can LEAD others to do the work. You become the lighthouse, and then you repeat the process all over again.

Take my current job, for example. I was working in Sacramento, installing a gas pipeline for PG&E down the middle of West Sacramento Avenue. Two city engineers came out to assist us in planning the traffic light timing and ensure certain electric lines were not energized. One city planner was a German immigrant who came to the US more than twenty years earlier and the other was a Polish immigrant who came to the US in search of a better life approximately ten years prior.

Learning of this, I said to the German native, "I have always wanted to tour Europe and see the old castles, churches, and aqueducts. Europe has a long history compared to the 243-year history the US has."

To which that son of a bitch said to me, "Yeah, 243 years of tainted history."

I replied, "We are the first country to allow you to work hard and keep what you earn."

And the GERMAN said, "Yeah, off the exploitation of those below you."

Apparently, Colonel Klink* was pissed off for some reason about the US. (And, unlike Hans Gruber here, I do not have a problem with having a boss. He obviously had taken the time to work and learn, but he never segued to leading and, by default, did not climb, move forward, and in no way could repeat.) Why he chose to move to the US is beyond me, because there are planes headed to Frankfurt every day.

I let my passion for the US get the better of me, and I bowed up on his condescending little face and said, "My boss drives a Bentley and has a private jet. Because he risked his money on this project, he can hire me, and I get to feed my family. I feel **employed, not exploited**! Furthermore, did the German native just stand here in broad daylight and say that US history is tainted? Last time I checked, the US didn't serialize, work to death, and try to exterminate an entire fucking religion!"

And that is when the biggest traffic flagger I've ever seen jumped between us and stopped that conversation from continuing. Seriously, she was like six feet three inches, had nails like Freddie Krueger, and a fucking "Stop-Proceed" sign in her hand. So, when she stepped between us and told us to stop, we listened. I glanced down at the Polish worker who was pulling wires and he smirked and shook his head. The Polish are not all that fond of the Germans, either.

---

* Colonel Klink was a character from the CBS sitcom, *Hogan's Heroes*.

The point of that anecdote was not that the US is better than Germany (although it is), but rather that the German guy was working his ass off to make ends meet and was pissed at the guys above him. He felt exploited, and the only reason was because he did not understand how to learn what was happening around him so he could eventually transition from a doer to a leader. He failed to pivot from someone who was doing what they were told because they're asked to by their boss to someone who knows why he is being asked to do it and understands his impact. He never MOVED ON from using his back to make money to using his head to make money.

But John, that's a load of crap because some of us don't have opportunity in our communities. That may be true, but you can buy a ticket and hop on a plane or a bus and move to some place where there is a more open market for your skill set. Bill Bucklew traveled from Tybee Island, Georgia, to Imperial Beach, California, ON FOOT! There are planes and buses leaving your city, state, or town every day. Go to where the money is! You won't be nearly as successful starting a scuba diving business in the Nevada desert as you would if you started it in Hawaii, right?

There are many examples of people who started off by doing the work and learning, and then transitioned into leading others. John Madden first played football for the Eagles and then eventually went on to become a commentator where he influenced others in the game. Mario Andretti went from being a longtime race car driver to owning a winery and a string of gas stations. Kim Kardashian went from making videos with Ray J in 2002 to working with the Pussycat Dolls in 2008 to making...umm, wait, on second thought, bad example there. Forget about Kim Kardashian. Clint Eastwood went from being an actor to becoming a director. Cindy Crawford went from modeling to owning and managing her own businesses. And the list goes on and on.

At the end of the day, if you choose to just do the job to make money your whole life without ever learning or moving on, that is fine. Lots of guys do it that way. But you should aspire to **keep moving forward** and **keep moving up**. Don't be content with simply doing your job. Do your job to the best of your ability, learn from it, and eventually lead it. Set your sights high and never look back.

When I got out of the Marines, I was told by many that I would be banging on the Marine Corps door begging to get back in. I was told I could never make it and that civilian life was very expensive. After all, besides working on the farm, at Burger King, and at a restaurant in high school, the Marines was all I knew, right? WRONG. I was tired of fixing CH46E helicopters, I was tired of listening to the officers use vocabulary words I did not know. I grew tired after more than six years of taking orders from guys who had been in the Corps less time than my bootlaces had. So, I did something about it.

And that is the point: Set your sights high and never look back. I didn't join the Boy Scouts to go camping, I joined to become an Eagle Scout. When I worked at Burger King, I did not just take orders, I made my best effort to have the highest ticket average. I did not join the service so my college education would be paid, I joined to challenge myself and chose to enlist in the Marines, which is the toughest branch to get into. I did not just go to college, I went to college to graduate with honors and high academic distinction, and I was awarded cum laude. I did not start off as a project engineer at Barnard Construction to simply be a solid employee, I wanted to make the most money possible and produce the best product (and to this day I have that reputation).

THE LAST CHAPTER: A CALL TO ACTION

This book is about getting the money you were born with from out of your head and ass. It is about telling life to fuck off with its roadblocks, and it is about making your life YOUR WAY! Screw the cannibals and their fucking canoes! It is about getting shit done and moving forward. It is about being resilient. Here is your call to action: Pick a goal, and remember: K.I.S.S. ("Keep It Simple, Stupid")!

Build the plan and execute it violently. I have spent the last several chapters describing how to accomplish your goals. I have provided five straightforward guidelines to help you get there. I have also provided examples of personal and mainstream triumphs, failures, and real and perceived roadblocks.

Now it's time to sit down and make a plan. Write it down in **simple, easy-to-understand terms.** Make the outline easy and quick to adjust on the fly as your situation evolves. This book started with just one page in a $3 notebook (see the next page).

The $2.9 billion Miami Dolphins team can't gain one yard without a $30 pigskin or the paint on the field. The simple things support all the other related luxuries and ancillary items in your day-to-day life, and the SIMPLE THINGS, when executed PROPERLY, will make your

41

✱ My Story: Book I don't
Steal Like an Artist.

✱ Rich. Sorgan+ gave me the title ✱

✱ My version of core four

✗ 4 Rules ~~5 Rules~~

"Rules"
Suck.

"5-fvid lines"

1 - No never means ~~not~~
2 - work hard to get lucky
3 - Remove Distractions
4 - Never know the best will
   Help of that you

Commit All rules

5 Know what you can change
+ what you can't.

Add To Book ➔ ✱ There is **NO best** ✱
   No Rules (Kinda)

not whiny

- het p @ 4:00am to
write for an Hour Every dy.
- Provide Examples of
   Triumph - failure - Obstacles
   etc.
- Be RAW ✱ (never complete)
- use pop culture (that's my References)
- Ask family + friends to be
   fucky Ruthless ➤ in their
   Evaluations of my writing.
- Keep it common Unpacked

✱ Last Chapter Resiliance.
call To Action ✱

success a reality. Practice them every day until they become habit, and keep doing them until they become a rote skill set.

I have a simple notebook where I write down my goals and tasks. Whenever I complete a task, I literally draw a line through it. I also update each task as it changes. This simple discipline gives me a sense of accomplishment in my day-to-day activities.

I developed the five guidelines because I understand one simple truth: There are in fact NO RULES for being successful. Outside of the laws that govern our country, there are no rules. When people tell you to think outside the box, what they are actually saying is that there is **no fucking box.**

The easiest way for you to get started is to buy a cheap notebook, or if you are so inclined, open up the notes app on your phone and put together a simple plan to build the next part of your life.

As you build your plan, return to these key principles:

1. Remember the five guidelines. Write them down—or tear out the sheet on page 81—and paste them on your mirror so you will see them first thing in the morning.

2. Know what you can do—and that is **anything you want!** There are NO RULES. Be as passionate as possible with every move you make!

3. There is no such thing as privilege. NEVER let anyone make you feel guilty for your work, your looks, your God, who you sleep with, or any other bullshit THEY create to make themselves feel better.

4. Build relationships with those around you in pursuit of your goals. Start with your wife or significant other. Work at this every day! NEVER STOP working to build better relationships.

5. Work, learn, and then master your tasks. No job is beneath you! Do what it takes.

6. Choose your clan and avoid the opinions of naysayers. You will be judged by others, but that will only matter if you allow yourself to care what they think. **Be sorry that you are not sorry for what they are fucking thinking.**

7. SHOW UP and do the work! Make your job easy! Set the table, so to speak; make the bed, set yourself up for success for the next day or the next task.

8. Be relentless in the pursuit of money every day.

Now you have a choice to make. You can choose either to be a TIGER or a ZEBRA. They both have stripes, but a tiger paves his own path, and sooner or later he has to eat.

Tear out this page and paste it where you will see it every day.

GUIDELINE #1:
"NO" NEVER MEANS "NO."

GUIDELINE #2:
WORK HARD TO GET LUCKY.

GUIDELINE #3:
REMOVE DISTRACTIONS.

GUIDELINE #4:
EVERY ROADBLOCK CAN HELP YOU.

GUIDELINE #5:
KNOW WHAT YOU CAN'T CHANGE
AND FOCUS ON WHAT YOU CAN CHANGE.

RESOURCES

MOVIES, TELEVISION, AND VIDEOS

Bress, Eric, and J. Mackye Gruber, dir. *The Butterfly Effect.* 2004; New Line Cinema.

Eastwood, Clint, dir. *The Outlaw Josey Wales.* 1976; Warner Bros.

Emmerich, Roland, dir. *Independence Day.* 1996; Twentieth Century Fox.

Game of Thrones. Directed by David Benioff, performance by Emilia Clarke and Kit Harington. Aired April 17, 2011. HBO.

Hell's Kitchen. Directed by Tony Croll, Brad Kreisberg, and Sharon Trojan Hollinger. Aired July 29, 2009. Fox Broadcasting Company.

Miller, Tim, dir. *Deadpool.* 2016; Twentieth Century Fox.

Ramis, Harold, dir. *Analyze This.* 1999; Warner Bros.

Ramis, Harold, dir. *Groundhog Day.* 1993; Columbia Pictures.

Shadyac, Tom, dir. *Bruce Almighty.* 2003; Universal Pictures.

Spielberg, Steven, dir. *Jurassic Park.* 1993; Universal Pictures.

Verbinski, Gore, dir. *Pirates of the Caribbean: The Curse of the Black Pearl.* 2003; Buena Vista Pictures.

YouTube. 2016. "Muscle Madness: PUSH the LIMITS with US Marine Veteran Jose Luis Sanchez." Last modified October 8. https://www.youtube.com/watch?v=NPjwymNNp78.

BOOKS

Whalen, Sean. 2018. *How to Make Sh*t Happen.* CreateSpace Independent Publishing Platform.

Willink, Jocko and Leif Babin. 2017. *Extreme Ownership.* New York: St. Martin's Press.

WEB PAGES AND ARTICLES

Biography. 2020. "Ben Carson Biography." Last modified January 14. https://www.biography.com/political-figure/ben-carson.

Deanna's Blog. 2016. "Ice Cream Sales Lead to Higher Homicide Rates: How Correlation Doesn't Always Equal Causation." Last modified August 16. https://www.egenerationmarketing.com/blog/causation-and-correlation-for-a-law-firm.

Jessen, Kenneth. 2012. "Former Slave Barney Ford Became a Colorado Millionaire." *Loveland Reporter-Herald*, February 24. Accessed February 20, 2019. https://www.reporterherald.com/2012/02/24/former-slave-barney-ford-became-a-colorado-millionaire-2/.

MLM Nation. 2003. "The Five People That Determine Your Income." https://mlmnation.com/the-five-people-that-determine-your-income-734/.

Yang, Stephanie. 2014. "Five Years Ago Bernie Madoff Was Sentenced to 150 Years in Prison—Here's How His Scheme Worked." *Business Insider*, July 1. https://www.businessinsider.com/how-bernie-madoffs-ponzi-scheme-worked-2014-7.

ACKNOWLEDGMENTS

I would like to take the time to acknowledge those closest to me, without whom this book would never have been possible.

First and foremost, to my loving wife, Jennifer. HSV, you are my proverbial lighthouse. You never waiver, and you are always there to shine your light and provide guidance for the MOTH. You have pushed me and made me a better man than I was before I met you. You have always managed to make time for me, and you pushed this former Marine when he required it. (That is no easy task.) You put up with my career choice, which forced you to move across the country thirteen times in under ten years, and you gave up your career to have a family with me. Furthermore, you have tirelessly managed the kids, pets, bills, and home life while you built and continue to run a profitable business as an entrepreneur. Thank you for being there for me and the kids, and for all that you have contributed to our family and this book. In my opinion, a better wife, partner, and best friend cannot be found.

And to my sister, Rose, who helped me proofread my manuscript. I know you took time away from your family and career to help me. Thank you for that, and for always showing up with a magic feather for your brother-rat. It seems like you are always there for me when I need someone to keep me sane over the years.

Thank you to my godmother, Aunt Kathi, who helped me edit my manuscript. You provided advice, you offered guidance, and you corrected a half-metric ton of spelling mistakes. Moreover, I know my style of writing is not your proverbial cup of tea, yet you took the time to help me anyway.

To my friend, Tyler. Thank you for helping me proofread my manuscript, and for co-writing the chapter on leadership. You literally tossed me a copy of the book, *Extreme Ownership*, and you lent me your phone for about two hours one day to introduce me to the book, *How to Make Sh*t Happen*. Then you took me to see Sean Whalen's seminar that following week. This influence has allowed me to connect things in life I would have been forever blind to, and it inspired me to write this book. I look forward to the next time we plant the Marine Corps flag on top of something we build.

Finally, thank you to Tim Barnard for allowing me to reference my experiences within your company in this book. Thank you for the leadership and career opportunity you have provided for me and my family. You have built an incredible company that is family-oriented and marries team effort with individual achievement.

There are many more people who have also influenced me over the years. Thank you to you all.

ABOUT THE AUTHOR

John Doerr is a father, husband, former US Marine Sergeant, inventor, author, and one of the founding members of the *Two Marine Dads* podcast. His drive has propelled his reputation as a master of self-reliance, adaptation, telling the hard truth, and capitalizing on every opportunity that comes his way.

He is a Florida-native farm boy who grew up dirt-poor and was classified at a young age as being Specific Learning Disabled. He has been beaten, stepped on, doubted, divorced, broke, arrested, torpedoed by those closest to him, and told he could never amount to anything. He has gone on to travel to over seventeen countries and has carved out a very good life for his family and himself. He has earned the Eagle Scout rank and the title of US Marine Sergeant. He has also earned his associate of arts degree and graduated cum laude from the University of North Florida with a bachelor of science in building construction.

John is a gun enthusiast and a whisky connoisseur, and when he is not scuba diving or wrenching on a vehicle, he can be found at home playing games with his three kids and hanging out with his wife.

TWO MARINE DADS PODCAST

Two Marine dads talking about the journey
of life, politics, kids, and family.

Listen and subscribe on Apple Podcast, Google,
Spotify, or wherever you get your podcasts.